HAMPSTEAD & BELSIZE PARK
THEN & NOW

IN COLOUR

MARIANNE COLLOMS & DICK WEINDLING

The History Press

First published in 2014

The History Press
The Mill, Brimscombe Port
Stroud, Gloucestershire, GL5 2QG
www.thehistorypress.co.uk

British Library Cataloguing in Publication Data.
A catalogue record for this book is available from the British Library.

ISBN 978 0 7509 5288 0

Typesetting and origination by The History Press
Printed in India.

CONTENTS

ACKNOWLEDGEMENTS

The authors would like to thank the staff of the Camden Local Studies and Archives Centre for their continuing help and co-operation. The Sainsbury Archive, Burgh House and Hampstead Museum, and Hopkins Architects kindly gave permission to use their images. Thanks are also due to Hampstead Community Centre.

Special thanks are due Roger Crocombe ARPS and Martin Colloms for taking the modern photographs.

Every effort has been made to contact the owners of the images reproduced in this book. All illustrations are copyright and reproduced with the kind permission of the following:

THE LONDON BOROUGH OF CAMDEN: Hampstead High Street [p.29]; Police Station, Rosslyn Hill [p.32]; Corner of Pond Street, South End Green, 1889 by H.L [p.46]; Belsize Branch Library [p.61].
BURGH HOUSE AND HAMPSTEAD MUSEUM: Stanfield House drawn by George Stanfield, [p.30]; Burgh House as Militia Headquarters [p.37]; Church Row tollgate [p.83].
THE SAINSBURY ARCHIVE, Museum of Docklands, Sainsbury shops, Heath Street [p.21].
HOPKINS ARCHITECTS: South Hampstead High School due to open in 2014 [p.75].
All other illustrations and photographs copyright of Marianne Colloms and Dick Weindling.

ABOUT THE AUTHORS

MARIANNE COLLOMS has co-authored a number of articles and books on the history of Camden, in particular Hampstead, Kilburn, Camden and Kentish Town. She is also a partner in a long-established design consultancy.

DICK WEINDLING was previously head of Educational Management at the National Foundation for Educational Research (NFER) and a freelance educational researcher. He is now retired and works on history projects with his writing colleague, Marianne Colloms. They are the authors of recent publications *Decca Studios and Klooks Kleek*, *Bloody British History: Camden* and *Camden Town and Kentish Town Then & Now*, also published by The History Press.

INTRODUCTION

This book shows the changing face of two north London neighbourhoods. In the early eighteenth century, Hampstead enjoyed not one but two brief episodes as a popular spa, with visitors coming to drink the unpleasant-tasting 'chalybeate' water. Georgian gems such as Church Row date from this period.

In 1814, Hampstead was described as 'a select, amicable, respectable and opulent neighbourhood' still some distance from London, with Belsize House and its pleasure gardens being another popular venue. Building development swept the house away in 1853, and Belsize Park developed into a 'pleasant airy suburb'.

Londoners came in their thousands to Hampstead Heath for the Bank Holiday fairs. The Vale of Health was a popular destination, as were pubs such as Jack Straw's Castle, the Bull & Bush and the Spaniards Inn. The Viaduct was part of an attempt to build on the Heath, which was widely resisted. A campaign was therefore mounted to save the Heath as an open space. The first area was secured in 1871, with subsequent additions, including Kenwood House, in the 1920s.

Hampstead and – to a lesser extent – Belsize Park attracted artists and writers. Many properties were built for the wealthy middle classes, but there were also streets that offered more modest homes, while early purpose-built housing for lower income families was provided by charitable individuals or trusts. Late 1880s improvements swept away alleys and narrow courts to extend Fitzjohn's Avenue to meet Heath Street as well as seeing the development of Hampstead Town Hall on Haverstock Hill (1877–78) and a hospital at Pond Street (1905). After delays and debate on station sites, the Hampstead Underground station opened in 1907. Shops and businesses were well established along Hampstead High Street and Heath Street by the early nineteenth century; other commercial centres developed in Belsize Park and along Finchley Road.

The 1930s saw the demolition of large properties, to be replaced by blocks of flats. Both neighbourhoods experienced bomb damage and loss of life during the Second World War, and in the post-war years, many houses were divided into flats. Hampstead and Belsize Park have experienced major redevelopment schemes in recent years, including the Royal Free Hospital (1974–78); the Finchley Road O2 centre (1998) and reworking of the Swiss Cottage leisure and library complex (2002–07). The rising cost of property exerts a great influence on the character and physical appearances of both neighbourhoods, while the debate of whether to demolish or rebuild and concern over the nature of some redevelopments continues. Today, Hampstead and Belsize Park have good transport links, a cosmopolitan population and both are still considered very good places to live.

THE SPANIARDS INN

CONSIDERED TO BE one of Hampstead's famous landmarks, the Spaniards Inn (on the right) is actually in the borough of Barnet, while the tollhouse across the road is in Camden.

The origin of the pub's name is unclear. Some sources believe it may come from Count de Gondomar, the Spanish Ambassador to James I, who lived in a house near here, known for complaining in a letter dated about 1620 that there was very little sun in England. A more likely source, though, is the Spanish landlord who was here in 1721.

The present building, with its many rooms and low ceilings, dates from the early eighteenth century. Hampstead was enjoying a period as a spa resort where Londoners came to take the waters. The Spaniards Inn became a popular destination; its pleasure gardens featured a bowling green and designs made of coloured pebbles on the walkways included the Tower of London, the Pyramids, and the Zodiac. Visitors could ascend a mound with views over the surrounding countryside, with claims to be able to see as far as Northamptonshire.

During the Gordon Riots in June 1780, a mob arrived at the Spaniards Inn armed with pitchforks, scythes, pokers and a few muskets. They planned to attack Lord Mansfield's Kenwood mansion. But the landlord of the Spaniards plied the rioters with drinks and sent for help while Lord Mansfield's steward handed out free beer. The militia arrived to find a drunken and disoriented rabble, which returned to London without any bloodshed. Charles Dickens, a frequent visitor, uses the story in *Barnaby Rudge* and he also describes the inn as the scene of merrymaking in *The Pickwick Papers*: Mrs Bardell was at the Spaniards tea gardens with friends when she was arrested for not having paid her bills.

Legend has it that highwayman Dick Turpin stabled his horse Black Bess here, with spare keys to the tollgate, allowing him to escape pursuers. Turpin was a bona fide highwayman, but links to the Spaniards are fictional, taken from William Harrison Ainsworth's 1834 novel *Rookwood*. He doesn't mention the pub, but claims that Turpin was chased from Kilburn to Hampstead Heath and over the Hornsey Tollgate. A building known as Dick Turpin's House, used as a tearoom, was demolished in 1934 and its site now lies under the car park.

The Spaniards Inn remains a popular destination. The protracted argument whether to demolish the crumbling tollhouse and widen the road was resolved when it was restored by the Hampstead Heath and Old Hampstead Society in 1967, with further work undertaken in 2011. Both buildings are Grade II listed.

THE OLD BULL & BUSH, NORTH END WAY

THIS PUB IN North End Way was popular long before it was made famous by the 1903 song 'Down at the Old Bull & Bush', performed by music hall entertainer Florrie Forde.

The pub may have developed from a seventeenth-century farmhouse and was probably named from the 'bull' of the farm and the ivy bush often used as a tavern sign. It's thought the painter William Hogarth once lived here; other artists who met and drank at the tavern included Joshua Reynolds and Thomas Gainsborough, who called it 'a delightful little snuggery'. Charles Dickens, Wilkie Collins and George du Maurier were also regulars. The postcard shows the entrance to the pub's famous gardens with its skittle alley, little arbours and band concerts.

In 1890 the pub was up for sale, described as a 'business of great magnitude and profit, from time immemorial the favourite rendezvous of the pleasure-seeking public. Never was it more popular or more prosperous than at the present moment'. A new publican even

kept caged monkeys in the garden. On Friday, 19 August 1898, two escaped and hid on Hampstead Heath, evading all pursuers tempted by a cash reward for their capture. On Monday, the monkeys gave themselves up, returning to the Bull & Bush, 'forlorn, dirty-looking, and evidently very miserable'. But within days they had escaped again, taking two more monkeys with them. The four explored Hampstead Heath between the Bull & Bush and the Spaniards Inn, damaging gardens and frightening residents. The publican reluctantly gave permission for the animals to be shot. Three were killed outright; the fourth, called Joey, was slightly wounded, and made his way back to his cage.

Hampstead-born Fred Vinall took over the pub around 1904. Son of the landlord of the Adelaide, Chalk Farm, he spent his working life in the licensing trade.

The current pub dates from 1924 but incorporates two older bay windows. Some rebuilding occurred after blast damage from a parachute bomb in 1940, and there have been several makeovers since. A car park has replaced the pleasure gardens and aside from the fact the pub is now called 'The Old Bull & Bush', all that remains to commemorate Florrie Forde are two life-size photos in the pub restaurant.

9

THE UPPER FLASK TAVERN, HEATH STREET

THIS DRAWING LOOKS south down Heath Street. The main building is the Upper Flask Tavern, dating from the early eighteenth-century spa years, when it was popular with visitors. It was also the summer meeting place of the elite Kit-Cat Club, whose eminent literary and artistic members shared Whig political beliefs, supporting the Protestant Hanoverian succession to the English throne. They included Sir Robert Walpole, William Congreve, Alexander Pope, Joseph Addison, Richard Steele and Sir George Kneller, who painted portraits of all forty-eight members. Architect and dramatist John Vanbrugh called it 'the best club that ever met'.

Samuel Richardson included the tavern in his 1748 novel *Clarissa* as the place where the tragic heroine was taken by the villain Lovelace. Soon after this, the Upper Flask became a private house, known as Upper Heath (later No. 194 Heath Street). George Steevens, the critic and Shakespearian authority, spent about £2,000 on the property, where he lived until his death in 1800.

The house was demolished after Lord Leverhulme gave the site to build Queen Mary's Maternity Home in 1922. Queen Mary often visited the Home as well as donating cot covers she had crocheted. Today, as Queen Mary's House, it is part of the Royal Free NHS Trust. From 1949 to 1983, the wide Heath Street pavement was used by the Hampstead Artists' Council for a popular open-air art market during summer weekends. It was criticised by local bookshop owner and author Ian Norrie in 1962, as 'no cause for local pride because the quality of work shown is generally so low'.

Across the road, modern houses have been built on the site of Heath Mount School. Evelyn Waugh was a pupil from 1910 to 1916, when the headmaster was J.S. Granville Grenfell, believed to be the model for the head in Waugh's *Decline and Fall* (1928). Other famous pupils at the school included Gerald du Maurier, the actor and father of author Daphne, and the photographer Cecil Beaton. Waugh remembered the young Beaton 'as a tender and very pretty little boy. My cronies and I tormented him ... our persecution went no further than sticking pins into him and we were soundly beaten for doing so.' The building was demolished in 1934 when a proposal to build a block of flats was defeated. The school moved to Hertfordshire.

FENTON HOUSE,
HAMPSTEAD GROVE

THIS IS THE oldest surviving mansion in Hampstead. The inscription '1693'
appears on a chimneystack but the house may date from around 1686.
The mansion was known as the Clock House for many years, after a timepiece
(since removed) over the current entrance. In 1706 it was bought by silk merchant
Joshua Gee who installed the elaborate wrought-iron gates facing Holly Hill. Gee
had close links with the American colonies; he was one of the mortgagees of
William Penn's property rights in Pennsylvania and a leading force in a partnership
that owned or controlled over 12,000 acres in North America. His colleagues
included Augustine Washington, father of George Washington.

In 1793, the mansion was bought by Philip Fenton, a Riga merchant, who
gave his name to the house. He moved in with his nephew and heir James along
with James' wife, Margaret, and their seven children. James probably relocated the
main entrance of the house to Hampstead Grove. He also helped fight Sir Thomas
Maryon Wilson's attempt to build on the Heath in 1829. The family remained in
the house until James' death aged 80, in 1834.

When Fenton House was put up for sale in 1884, little was said about its history; rather it was described as 'immediately ripe for development and suitable for the erection of good class houses'. Fortunately new owner George Careless Trewby was looking for a family home. He was the chief engineer of the Gas, Light and Coke Company and was largely responsible for building the largest gasworks in Europe at Beckton, on the banks of the Thames. Trewby was on hand in 1878, when the *Princess Alice* pleasure steamer collided with a collier on the river opposite Beckton. It sank with great loss of life but he managed to rescue four people. Trewby served as a churchwarden at nearby Christchurch and died at Fenton House in 1910.

In 1920, the property was withdrawn from auction at £17,500, having failed to meet its reserve. Fenton House and its 'beautiful old-world grounds' were bequeathed to the National Trust by its last owner, Lady Binning, in 1952. The house opened to the public the following year. The objects decorating the rooms are a mix of her acquisitions and those of her mother and uncle. The Benton Fletcher collection of early keyboard instruments is also on display, and in addition to concerts, these instruments are sometimes played to entertain visitors.

ROMNEY'S HOUSE, HOLLY BUSH HILL

THE BUILDING ON Holly Hill that was home to the Hampstead Constitutional Club in 1910 today carries a blue plaque to artist George Romney. A regular visitor to Hampstead, in 1796 he bought a large property with the intention of converting it into a house, studio and space to display statues and pictures. He pulled down the stables and coach house on Holly Hill and began building, commuting daily to his London house in Cavendish Square. His son believed a studio could easily have been added to the original house and was appalled to find his father had spent nearly £3,000 on his new home. Romney moved to Hampstead in December 1798, before the house was completed. Many paintings had to be stored outside; some were stolen and others were damaged by the weather. It proved too much for the artist, who fell into a deep depression and left to join his wife in Kendal, dying there in 1802.

Famous for his portraits, Romney painted Nelson's mistress Lady Emma Hamilton on more than sixty occasions. Several Romney portraits are on display at nearby Kenwood House, including several of Emma.

A large part of the property, now called 'Romney's House', was built after he died but part of his home – greatly altered – probably remains. In 1806, the house was sold to the Trustees of the Hampstead Assembly Rooms, to become a cultural centre for Hampstead, 'the village for some years past being without any fit place for balls, dinners and other public entertainments'. They commissioned a new tearoom and ballroom. Romney's stable was demolished and rebuilt as the Holly Bush Tavern, originally linked to the Assembly Rooms as a catering wing.

In 1829, the first Hampstead Heath Protection meeting was held in the Assembly Rooms, chaired by James Fenton of neighbouring Fenton House. In 1833 a series of lectures was given by famous speakers of the day including Michael Faraday, John Constable and Elizabeth Fry. In about 1931, the building was sold to Clough William-Ellis, the architect of Portmerion in North Wales. He said: 'The fine old house, being far too large either for our needs or means ... was proportionately delightful to inhabit ... a splendid house for large parties.' William-Ellis sold the house to Raymond Russell, a collector of musical instruments. Recently the property, now a private residence, has been extensively refurbished but externally, the appearance of the Holly Hill frontage and adjacent terrace remains largely unaltered.

NEW END HOSPITAL

OPENED IN 1729, the first workhouse stood where Mount Vernon is today. By 1877, it housed around eighty paupers. In 1801, they were transferred to a house at New End that in turn was replaced by a third, purpose-built workhouse, opened in 1848. The building designed by H.E. Kendall is shown on the postcard below. Run by the Hampstead Vestry (local authority), the inmates had to earn their keep. 'Everyone who can work at all is set to do something.' Breaking stones for road mending was one task: fragments had to be small enough to pass through a grid on the workshop window. Some paupers were apprenticed to traders.

A workhouse infirmary was built in 1869–70, enlarged in 1878 and again in 1883–85, from the plans of Charles Bell. He designed an innovative circular building with three floors of wards, a central ventilation shaft and nurses' accommodation on the top floor. A water tower holding 12,000 gallons was included. By 1905, the workhouse had been extended as far as Heath Street. Inquests were held here and the building was used by the Vestry until the Town Hall was built on Haverstock Hill.

In 1915, the workhouse became a military hospital, and after the end of the First World War, renamed as New End Hospital. It was taken over by the London County Council (LCC) in 1929–30, becoming a general hospital with 260 beds. A maternity unit was opened, plus casualty and outpatient departments. New End Hospital was absorbed by the newly established National Health Service in 1948 and became a pioneering centre for thyroid surgery. When Ruth Ellis shot her lover David Blakely outside the Magdala pub at South End Green in 1955, he was rushed to New End Hospital but pronounced dead on arrival. The hospital's last role, from 1974 until it closed in 1985, was as the geriatric unit of the Royal Free Hospital.

There was a lengthy debate over the site's future. While some favoured demolition, in the mid-1990s it was agreed to preserve the main frontage while refurbishing many of the buildings, including the circular wards, for private residential use. The mortuary (a separate building opposite the hospital) was converted to become the New End Theatre in 1974, closing in 2011, when the premises became the Village Shul.

THE FRIENDS' MEETING HOUSE, HEATH STREET

THIS 1911 SKETCH shows from left to right, Nos 120 to 110 Heath Street. Paying £1,000 for the site to build their meeting house, the Quakers noted that 'prices rule high in Hampstead'. Designed by Frederick Rowntree for a fee of £120, it opened in November 1907. The 'freestyle Arts and Crafts' building features a curved, copper-roofed porch and attractive entry gates. Behind the meeting house, the spire of Christchurch, built in 1852, is just visible. Two of the neighbouring properties had been occupied by the same family businesses for sixty years: Borley the grocers (No. 116) and Hammond the butchers (No. 112).

Their name is on the shop awning in the sketch. Gardener John Philpot Jones lived at the ivy-covered Mansfield Cottage (No. 118) for over forty years: from 1879 to 1887 his lodger was the reclusive Henry Sweet, phonetician and philologist. Bernard Shaw called Sweet 'the greatest English phonetician of his time' and it is said that he partly modelled his character, Professor Higgins, in *Pygmalion* on Sweet.

The terrace is clearly recognisable in the modern photo. A narrow alley, Stamford Close, still runs between Nos 114 and 116. There were six cottages behind the shops, home to fifty people in 1871. In 1934, the properties were described as occupying a 'miserable dark square – a black spot', and condemned by the Hampstead Council. Today, all the Heath Street properties, with the exception of No. 116, are listed Grade II.

SAINSBURY'S SHOPS, Nos 41 AND 45, HEATH STREET

GROCER JOHN SAINSBURY lived over his first shop at No. 173 Drury Lane, opened in 1869. More shops followed in the suburbs. In the late 1880s, Fitzjohn's Avenue was extended from Perrins Lane through a jumble of streets and alleys to the junction of Heath and Hampstead High Streets. A number of new, modern shops were built, including No. 45 Heath Street, which opened as 'John Sainsbury provision merchants' in 1895. The second shop at No. 41 followed much later, in 1955. They were separated by Boots chemists, who took over an existing chemist's shop in around 1902. An elaborate leaded window at first-floor level illuminated their subscription library. The scheme was set up by Florence, the wife of business founder Jesse Boot, and customers paid to borrow books.

In January 1955, Sainsbury opened 'Happy Hampstead's new shop,' in response to a steadily increasing volume of trade.

Appropriately enough, the manager was a Mr Heath. The shop at No. 45 had a makeover at the same time and both branches now displayed the ultra-modern glass shopfronts. The shops were tiled white from floor to ceiling. Fresh meat was jointed and packed behind the shop, with non-perishable goods stored in the basement. As the photograph shows, customers were happy to leave their babies outside in their prams.

Both shops had counters running the length of their walls with a cash desk at the far end. According to local residents, 'each counter had its own function – dairy goods on one, meat on another, dried goods and household goods at the others. At the dairy counter, butter was rolled and patted, and wrapped in greaseproof paper; cheese was cut by wire from huge rounds.' Shopping was a more leisurely pastime then. 'After completing purchases from one counter, customers had to go to the back of the queue for purchases from another counter.' To save time, children would be sent to save a place for their mother in another queue. 'Everything was sold loose and by weight, and had to be scrupulously measured out and wrapped.' No bags were provided; customers brought their own.

Sainsbury closed both shops in 1970. At the time, the company was closing many branches if they weren't big enough to be turned into the new style 'self-service' stores. Today the shopfronts have been remodelled but the Boots subscription library windows are still in place at No. 43, which has traded as a chemist for over 100 years.

HAMPSTEAD
HIGH STREET

THIS VIEW LOOKS north up Hampstead
High Street to the fire station tower at the corner
of Holly Hill. The shops on the left-hand side
replaced older premises demolished in the late
1880s, when the High Street was widened as
part of local improvements. Opposite, a London
General Omnibus Company horse bus is waiting
outside the Bird in Hand pub. In 1890 there was
a fifteen-minute service; a bus carried twenty-six
passengers, twelve inside and fourteen outside,
costing 1*d* for a short ride and 4*d* for the entire
journey. The bus depot was in the yard behind
the pub, providing stabling for 100 horses: with
changes, twelve horses were needed daily to service
each bus. Uphill from the pub, three oil jars at
first-floor level advertise a long-established oil and
colourman business, selling general hardware items

as well as oils for lamps, pigments and dyes for paint. Across the street was George Gaze at No. 66. Aged 50 and a successful Fulham draper, his doctor advised him to retire and go to live 'on higher ground'. He decided to move to Hampstead but he kept on working, acquiring a bankrupt business and later expanding to occupy No. 65 as well.

A local resident recalled her 1920s childhood. By this time, Gaze also sold clothes and haberdashery. 'There were the cosy, family-type ladies and gentleman in Gaze's, where we bought my Liberty bodices and the buttercup, daisy, poppy and cornflower wreaths for my summer hats. My governess tried on her stays in the private and mysterious recesses behind the curtains at the back of the shop.' The shop became a Hampstead institution: 'a neighbour declared that if Gaze's went, she would die'. The two photos show how little the buildings have changed save for new shop fronts, but today, few of the High Street businesses cater for day-to-day needs. The ironmongers closed in 1979 and Gaze followed the following year. The bird in hand carving is still visible on the exterior of the first floor, but the pub shut in the mid-1980s, reopening as a restaurant.

FLASK WALK

FLASK WALK, ONE of the oldest streets in Hampstead, originally led to the spa buildings in Well Walk. The entrance was spanned by a two-storey building that collapsed in 1911, and its name probably derives from the flasks used to carry the spa water. This photograph was taken in the mid-1950s, when the shops included three butchers and two greengrocers. Elsie Hooper ran the the Flask Pharmacy (No. 1) for over thirty years, closing in the 1960s. The Taylor's fish and chip shop (Nos 5–7) was very popular, and Mrs Spearey's sweetshop at No. 4 (displaying the 'Players Please' advert) was another favourite, with, as her daughter Pat recalls: 'display counters on two sides and wall-shelves for dozens of glass sweet jars: toffees, sherbet lemons, liquorice, chocolate drops, dolly mixture, [and] jelly babies.' Like Sainsbury's shops, everything was sold by weight. Green & Son electric dealers occupied No. 11, but in the 1920s it was run as a clothes shop by Miss Goff. Local resident John Price remembered it clearly: 'Whatever time of day or year, the shop was in semi-gloom; across the two counters were various pieces of string on which items of clothing were displayed – socks, vests, pants and suchlike.'

This end of Flask Walk, which originally carried two-way traffic, was pedestrianised in 1972. It appears in many paintings by Charles Ginner, a member of the Camden Town Group of artists. He lived opposite, above No. 61 Hampstead High Street. The Flask pub (No. 14) was trading as a beerhouse by the early 1700s and is one of the oldest drinking establishments in Hampstead. The water from the nearby spa, praised for its medicinal qualities, was bottled and sold here, while a visitor could take rooms and stable his horse

nearby. The present building dates from 1874–75 and still has Victorian glass panels in its entry doors and above the partition that separates the bars, plus a series of five attractive Victorian chromolithographs. Services on offer have adapted to the passing years. An oyster bar has long since disappeared, while a ground-floor skittle alley gave way to a billiards room and finally the current lounge bar. During renovations in 1990, the landlord said, 'The Flask is not one of those plastic places with a jukebox. The only sounds you hear are those of people enjoying themselves.' The famous 'Flask chip' even won a mention in the *Good Food Guide*. Apparently, cutting the potatoes by hand, not machine, was the secret.

ROWLAND SMITH AND THE POST OFFICE, 77–81 HAMPSTEAD HIGH STREET

PICTURED SHORTLY BEFORE closing in the late 1960s, the photograph shows Rowland Smith's 'rambling old showrooms' on Hampstead High Street. The firm started in the 1920s with a single unit and progressively took over adjoining properties to occupy Nos 77–81a. Rowland's father George manufactured and sold cycles and what he called 'motors'. Rowland built a very successful business, trading in second-hand motorcycles, combinations and 'light cars' with less than 1.5-litre engine capacity. The firm advertised widely and paid cash on the spot. New cars were sold from a showroom opposite (Nos 25 and 26). At various times, the firm also occupied

garage and workspaces in Heath Street, Perrin's Walk, Flask Walk and the Vale of Health. A local resident remembered 'the clusters of furtive salesmen who brought a more clandestine aspect to the area'. All of the High Street property was put up for sale in 1963, withdrawn, and then remarketed in 1967.

Camden Council now own Nos 77 and 78. The plan was to open No. 77 as a library, but instead it houses Hampstead Community Centre and a florist. The Post Office paid £100,000 for Nos 79–81a. Concerns were raised that a high block 'would destroy the balance of the street by looming too large', and that the replacement needed 'a personality all its own yet not so strident as to demand undue attention'. A low build was agreed and the current post office by J. E. Jolly was opened in 1974. Unfortunately, it found little favour with Sir Nikolaus Pevsner, who described it as 'insensitive' in his *Buildings of England* series.

Rowland Smith's London home was in the Hampstead Garden Suburb but he spent time in Devon, where he owned the Palace Hotel in Torquay and the nearby Coleton Fishacre estate (acquired by the National Trust in 1982). Smith died in 1979 and left £3.5 million (worth about £15 million today).

HAMPSTEAD HIGH STREET

THIS EARLY PHOTOGRAPH from the 1860s, taken from outside
Stanfield House, looks north up Hampstead High Street. The unbroken
run of premises opposite predates the building of Gayton Road in 1870.
This meant demolishing the shops occupied by plumber Daniel Simon
(No. 20) and confectioner John Tanner (No. 21), which are the third
and fourth premises from the right in the photo. Part of No. 22 was also
demolished (shielded by the awning).

In the 1920s and '30s, No. 23 was an antique shop, run by Lisette
Pyett. Local author Eleanor Farjeon was a regular customer and
enthused about the many bargains she bought. 'The window was an
endless source of wonder, littered with medleys of silver and trinkets
and china, lace and embroideries, ornaments and small curios of all
descriptions.' The interior was densely packed with furniture, glass,
china, jewels and weaponry: 'there wasn't an object you didn't want
to handle.'

In the 1890s, No. 27 became Knowles Brown, jewellers. The centrepiece of the window display for over eighty years was an Austrian mechanical clock in the shape of a dog. It stuck out its tongue and wagged its tail every second; an endless source of fascination for passing children. The shop eventually closed on Christmas Eve 1984.

No. 29 was occupied by a number of medical men over the years, including a Dr Rodd, who attended local resident John Keats after the poet suffered a minor haemorrhage. Edward Blanchard Stamp opened a 'high class dispensing and manufacturing business' on the premises, but soon after he arrived, the shop was gutted by fire in 1870. The rebuilding incorporated external decorations of medicinal plants and flowers. Stamp made many of his dispensing compounds on the premises and he also manufactured products such as Myrrhine Toothpaste, Parrish's Chemical Food (an iron tonic) and Pernisfuge, claimed to be a 'certain cure for chilblains'. He left his mark on Hampstead in the tiled entrance to his shop, which still reads 'Stamp Chemist'.

Today all these shops are clothes retailers, as are the two shops (extreme right in the old photo), which are now the first and second premises south of Gayton Road. Just round the corner in 1901, No. 61 Gayton Road was the home of 18-year-old Ethel le Neve, later to gain notoriety as the mistress of Dr Crippen.

STANFIELD HOUSE

THIS IS ANOTHER group of properties partly destroyed by road building. Built around 1730, the painting shows ivy covered Stanfield House in its original terrace setting. Two houses were demolished when Prince Arthur Road was built around 1871, but Stanfield House survived as the corner property on the new street, as shown in the modern photo.

The house is named after artist Clarkson Stanfield R.A, best known for his nautical paintings and highly realistic theatrical scenery. His son George produced the painting shown here. Clarkson moved to Hampstead from Camden Town in 1847. One of his closest friends and frequent visitors was Charles Dickens, who described 'dear old Stanny' as 'the soul of frankness, generosity and simplicity ... the most genial, the most affectionate and the most lovable of men'. Stanfield left Hampstead for No. 6 Belsize Park Gardens in 1865, and died there two years later.

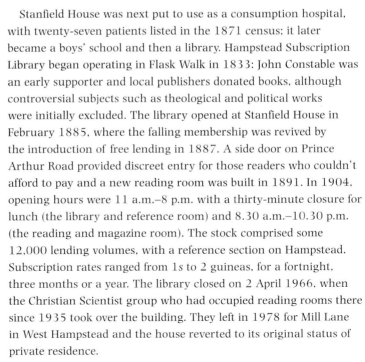

Stanfield House was next put to use as a consumption hospital, with twenty-seven patients listed in the 1871 census; it later became a boys' school and then a library. Hampstead Subscription Library began operating in Flask Walk in 1833: John Constable was an early supporter and local publishers donated books, although controversial subjects such as theological and political works were initially excluded. The library opened at Stanfield House in February 1885, where the falling membership was revived by the introduction of free lending in 1887. A side door on Prince Arthur Road provided discreet entry for those readers who couldn't afford to pay and a new reading room was built in 1891. In 1904, opening hours were 11 a.m.–8 p.m. with a thirty-minute closure for lunch (the library and reference room) and 8.30 a.m.–10.30 p.m. (the reading and magazine room). The stock comprised some 12,000 lending volumes, with a reference section on Hampstead. Subscription rates ranged from 1s to 2 guineas, for a fortnight, three months or a year. The library closed on 2 April 1966, when the Christian Scientist group who had occupied reading rooms there since 1935 took over the building. They left in 1978 for Mill Lane in West Hampstead and the house reverted to its original status of private residence.

HAMPSTEAD POLICE STATION AND VANE HOUSE, ROSSLYN HILL

HAMPSTEAD WAS PART of the 'S' division of the Metropolitan Police Force and they moved local headquarters several times. In 1868, they left their station on the corner of Holly Hill and Heath Street (later rebuilt as the fire station) for this building on Rosslyn Hill, pictured here left of the middle two trees. There was accommodation onsite for the station inspector, his family and an average complement of twenty unmarried police constables. Hampstead Heath created its own problems for the local constabulary, from suicides in the ponds to lost children at the many fairs. On Whit Monday 1890, ten unclaimed youngsters were forced to spend the night at the police station!

Shown behind the police station and approached through the metal gates was the charitable Royal Soldiers' Daughters' Home, occupying a remodelled and extended Vane House. There was a separate school building. The girls moved here in 1858, marching uphill from their first home in Belsize Park, wearing their distinctive red dresses. The charity began during the Crimean War 'for the maintenance, clothing, and education of the daughters of soldiers'. Girls were given skills to equip them for domestic service: taught to make and mend clothes, to help in the kitchen, sick room and nursery. To this end, they carried out the home's housework, washing and ironing.

By 1890, the home had trained over 1,000 girls as domestic servants, while some were helped to better occupations. When girls left, they were given a trunk containing useful items such as dresses, stockings, boots and an umbrella. Renamed the Royal Soldiers' Daughters' School (RSDS) in 1946, it remained in Vane House until the late 1960s. The separate school building was sold in 1951 and now forms part of Fitzjohn's Primary School. In the meantime, the police had moved again in 1913, to the corner of Rosslyn Hill and Downshire Hill. That station closed in 2013.

The film *Les Bicyclettes de Belsize* (1968) gives a fleeting glimpse of the old Rosslyn Hill police station before it and Vane House were both demolished. A new RSDS was built, with private housing on the remainder of the site. In 2012, the RSDS closed and leased its buildings to North Bridge House School. Amazingly, the low wall along Rosslyn Hill has survived, along with the brick entrance piers to Vane House.

ROSSLYN HILL CHAPEL AND THE ROSSLYN ARMS

THE OLD NAME for Rosslyn Hill was Red Lion Hill, named after a pub on the site of the police station. The photograph below was taken in the late 1890s before the two shops on the left (Nos 52 and 50) were demolished. They were long-established businesses: by 1861, the Camps were selling fruit and vegetables from No. 50 and a few years later, the Woodwards took over a stationery and bookseller's business at No. 52. Both families lived above their shops.

Founded in 1692, the present Rosslyn Hill Unitarian Chapel opened in 1862, and has been progressively enlarged and remodelled. Access was from Pilgrim's Lane but Dr Brooke Herford, who took over as minister in 1892, believed there should be an

entrance facing Rosslyn Hill. In 1898, the congregation bought Nos 50 and 52, the shops were demolished and the present entry was created. The Rosslyn Arms was built in 1869, replacing the pub across the road, which had been demolished to build the police station.

Today, Rosslyn Hill Chapel is clearly signed, the building approached along a wide path from the main road. The entry from Pilgrims Lane was sold to developers in 1953. Pevsner, in his *Buildings of England*, notes that the 'furnishings and monuments of high quality indicate the strength of Hampstead Unitarianism'. There is some good Victorian glass, including windows by Henry Holiday, Sir Edward Burne-Jones and William Morris. Next door, the pediment bearing the date 1869 has disappeared from the Rosslyn Arms. In the 1930s, some of the chapel congregation suggested displaying temperance posters on noticeboards next to the pub, but this was considered too provocative. The pub was then known for its excellent seafood, the landlord buying fresh supplies from Billingsgate Market every morning. In the 1960s, the publicans Henry and Sheila Martin were very popular with their regulars, 'content to let it be the customer's pub as much as theirs'. The Rosslyn Arms is currently closed.

BURGH HOUSE

BURGH HOUSE DATES from about 1703. Down the years the building has been extended by its owners, many of whom played a prominent role in Hampstead life. In 1720, it was occupied by Dr William Gibbons, the first doctor to promote the restorative powers of the chalybeate water on sale at the nearby spa. In 1822, the Revd Allatson Burgh, vicar of St Lawrence Jewry, bought the house for £2,546 and gave his name to the property. Burgh House was in military hands from 1858 to 1881 as the headquarters and officers' mess for the Royal East Middlesex Militia. A turnout is shown in the old photograph.

Reverting to a private residence, there followed a series of tenants and owners. Thomas Grylls (1884–98) designed and made stained glass. Dr George Williamson (1906–24) commissioned Gertrude Jekyll to design the garden. Captain Constantine Evelyn Benson, DSO and banker, bought the property for £4,750 in 1925.

The last private occupants were George and Elsie Bainbridge. Elsie was Rudyard Kipling's daughter. In 1934 he cautioned her that Hampstead rates were very high but went on, 'all reports unite in saying 'tis a most beautiful house and garden – a big garden as,

doubtless, you know'. The couple left in 1937 and the house was again put up for sale. Amazingly, Burgh House survived a bombing raid in the Second World War that damaged many adjacent properties. In 1945, Hampstead Council compulsorily purchased these and other houses in Well Walk and New End with the aim of redeveloping the area as social housing. It agreed to preserve Burgh House and open up the view to Well Walk, but most of the property's 1-acre garden planted with 'roses, rhododendrons; lilac, azalea, clematis, japonica, wisteria and mature trees' was taken and all that remains today is a small terrace. In 1979, Camden Council granted a lease of the property to the Burgh House Trust; in September of that year, the house opened as a local centre and Hampstead Museum. Facilities have recently been upgraded and refurbished with the help of lottery money.

WELL WALK AND HAMPSTEAD SPA

THE PAINTING SHOWS Well Walk looking towards the Heath. In the
early eighteenth century, the small village of Hampstead was enjoying
its first spell as a spa, popularly referred to as 'Hampstead Wells'.
The Hampstead Wells Trust owned 6 acres bordering on Well Walk,
including the spa spring. Their lessee built the Long Room (the large
building on the right), comprising a pump room where visitors drank
the water piped from the nearby spring, and the large Assembly Room,
where regular concerts and dances were held. The health benefits of
drinking the unpleasant tasting chalybeate water (which contained iron)
were vigorously promoted by Dr Gibbons of Burgh House, who consumed
several glasses daily. Pleasure grounds with a pond and bowling green
opened behind the Long Room. Unfortunately, the spa's success attracted
a growing number of disreputable visitors: 'so many loose women that
modest company are ashamed to appear here', cautioned John Macky's
A Journey Through England (1714). The rise in popularity of Belsize House
further contributed to the decline of the Wells. In 1725, the Long Room
was converted into a chapel, with pews, a gallery and organ. This role

lasted until 1862, when the 3rd Middlesex (Hampstead) Rifle Volunteers took over the building as a drill hall.

Hampstead Wells Trust was legally bound to use its income and profits 'for the benefit and advantage of the poor of Hampstead'. The trustees drew up plans to develop their property, and, in 1882, the Long Room was demolished. Its site is now partially covered by the entrance to Gainsborough Gardens, where properties and a communal garden were laid out on the spa's pleasure ground. The spring is now covered by Nos 6–8 Well Road. The ivy-covered house with attractive windows survived as No. 46 Well Walk. The basin where a girl is filling her pitcher was replaced by a drinking fountain in 1882, at a cost of £179. In 1904 a resident commented: 'This new fountain drips drop by drop very slowly, and never has done otherwise. Persons in the early morning may still be seen endeavouring to obtain a small quantity of it. It is said to form an excellent lotion for weak eyes.' Subsequent analysis revealed the water was unfit for drinking and a new supply was introduced in 1907. The fountain was restored and re-commissioned in 1978 and again in 1997, but it is currently dry.

WILLOW ROAD AND ERNŐ GOLDFINGER

THESE FOUR EIGHTEENTH-CENTURY cottages were eventually designated Nos 1–4
Willow Road, No. 1 being adjacent to the garden of the Freemasons' Arms on
Downshire Hill. Previously they were variously known as (Lower) Heath Cottages, Willow
Place and Willow Cottages, and they faced Hampstead Heath. The postcard dates from the
early twentieth century, with Alfred Farn in No. 4, 'electrical lighting, heating, cooking,
bells & telephones' and Miss Eliza Webster, laundress, next door. Eliza was living here
with her parents in 1851 (when she was just 1 year old) and she was still in her cottage
sixty-five years later. In 1936, the LCC refused to grant permission to Hungarian-born
architect Ernő Goldfinger to demolish the cottages and replace them with a block of flats.
His modern terrace of three houses, 'conceived as a contemporary echo of the Georgian
terraces round the corner in Downshire Hill' was, however, allowed. Designed to appear as

a single building, the intention was to create a double-width family home for Goldfinger, flanked by a smaller house for a friend and another to be sold to help finance the project.

The plans for the terrace, which has a concrete frame with brick-faced external walls, raised a storm of local protest. Complaints of a 'modern angular house in reinforced concrete' were dismissed by supporters who argued, 'as for the objection that the houses are rectangular, only the Eskimos and the Zulus build anything but rectangular houses'. Author Ian Fleming opposed the build, and it is said this prompted him to name his famous villain and James Bond adversary, 'Goldfinger'. Ernő's home – No. 2 – in the centre of the terrace has pure lines and flowing spaces, where he designed the fittings and most of the furniture. Regarded today as a 'visionary' architect, at the time his work was often controversial; Alexander Fleming House (now Metro Central Heights) at the Elephant and Castle and Trellick Tower in Ladbroke Grove are among his better-known designs.

Ernő Goldfinger died in 1987 and his widow in 1991, still living at Willow Road. A successful appeal was raised by the National Trust to buy the house from Ernő's heirs, who had agreed to donate the contents. This was one of the first modernist buildings acquired by the Trust and was opened to the public in 1996.

41

KEATS HOUSE,
KEATS GROVE

BORN IN 1795, John Keats entered medical school in 1815, around the time two friends, Charles Armitage Brown and Charles Wentworth Dilke, decided to build a house on today's Keats Grove. Wentworth Place was in fact two properties designed to look like a single house, having a shared kitchen and a common garden. After being introduced to Leigh Hunt's literary circle in the Vale of Health in 1816, Keats decided to abandon medicine for poetry. He and his brother Tom rented rooms in Well Walk until Tom died of tuberculosis in 1818, whereupon Keats moved in with Brown at Wentworth Place. Dilke had already introduced Keats to Fanny Brawne and they fell in love. He wrote many of his most important poems in 1819, including 'Ode to a Nightingale', inspired by a nesting bird in the garden, or perhaps, hearing a nightingale on the Heath. In February 1820, Keats caught a severe chill riding home on the outside of the Hampstead coach. When Keats coughed up blood, Brown summonsed the surgeon on Hampstead High Street, but the poet knew the signs of TB and said, 'that is my death-warrant'. Advised to seek warmer climes, he left England for Italy in September 1820 and died in Rome on 23 February 1821. Fanny Brawne mourned Keats for many years, before marrying in 1833.

Eventually renamed Lawn Bank, the house passed through the hands of many owners and occupiers, including artists Henry Courtney Selous and Robert Scott Temple; retired actress and one-time mistress of George IV, Eliza Chester, who made the two properties into one, adding the single-storey extension; piano maker Charles Cadby and physiologist Dr William Sharpey. In 1896, a plaque commemorating John Keats was fixed above the front door. A committee raised funds to buy the house when it was threatened with demolition in 1920, much of the cash raised in America. Hampstead Council agreed to take over the property and Keats (Memorial) House opened to the public in 1925. In 1931, a combined Keats Memorial Library and Keats Museum opened next door, on the site of the old stables. This became a branch library after the Second World War, when it was decided to move the collection of Keats memorabilia into the newly renovated Keats House. The house is now the responsibility of the City of London. The library was shut by Camden Council in March 2012 and reopened as Keats Community Library, a volunteer-run charity.

HAMPSTEAD HEATH STATION, SOUTH END ROAD

THE POSTCARD DATES from the turn of the twentieth century and looks towards South End Green. Hampstead Heath station opened on 2 January 1860, having staircases to both platforms and a ticket collector's booth at the bottom of each staircase. From the outset, the station was well used by Londoners, who flocked to ''Appy 'Ampstead' at weekends and Bank Holidays. By 1884, the Whitsun and Easter fairs had spread from the Green, past the station and up the hill to the Vale of Health and Spaniards Road. Stalls and barrows lined the roadsides. On Easter Monday, 18 April 1892, about 19,000 adults and children arrived at the station. The weather became unsettled towards 6 p.m. and many decided to call it a day. They piled into the station and down the stairs for City-bound trains. It's likely someone

fell, causing an obstruction, and the ticket booth created a bottleneck. Two women and six boys were crushed to death. A medical student saw the boys 'wedged up in a corner behind the box' and two women 'struggling frantically', all going blue in the face.

Some injured passengers were taken to Hampstead Workhouse infirmary and the dead to the mortuary. The inquest returned a verdict of accidental death by suffocation, the youngest victim being 9-year-old John Connor from Camden Town. The official enquiry ruled that the station was unfit to deal with large crowds, agreeing with James Hewetson, a vestryman and Hampstead bookseller, who told the inquest the railway company had been asked on several occasions to upgrade the station and its approaches to deal with the great increase in passenger numbers. In June 1892, a London paper reported that many modifications had been carried out; in particular, the booths had been removed. In the 1960s the line was saved from closure when the station was rebuilt and the bridge widened in 1968. In 2007, the line became part of London Overground, launched here by Ken Livingstone, the Mayor of London, on 12 November. Currently the station is being renovated. Still popular with visitors to the Heath, it also provides essential access to the Royal Free Hospital, whose buildings (background, right) dwarf the landscape.

POND STREET AND
SOUTH END GREEN

THIS PAINTING SHOWS the buildings at the corner of Pond Street and South End Road. There was a dairy here for many years, selling milk from cows that grazed nearby on South End Farm. By 1889, it was Edmund Goodman's grocery shop, with chickens wandering safely in the roadway outside. Goodman later ran a coffee stall on the opposite side of the Green.

The premises became No. 1 South End Road, occupied for many years by a second-hand bookshop, Booklover's Corner. In 1934 and 1935, George Orwell lived in a flat over the shop, selling books in the afternoon to help pay the rent. He wrote about his experiences in a 1936 essay called 'Bookshop Memories' and also in his novel *Keep the Aspidistra Flying*, published the same year. Orwell's time at the shop was commemorated by a plaque beside the door that included a bas-relief of his face, but this was stolen in 2010.

In the 1950s, the shop became the Prompt Corner Café, a Hampstead institution through to the mid-1980s. For the price of a cup of coffee, customers could spend the whole day playing chess. Today the shop is a bakery and restaurant.

The drinking fountain on the right was donated by Anne Crump in 1880 and stands on the site of the pond that gave the street its name. She was a relative of the owner of Hereford House, which stood opposite. Demolished in 1913, flats and a supermarket now occupy its site. Anne wanted to provide refreshment for visitors, to 'help stop intemperance and vice'. In 2006–07, a restoration project enhanced the area around the fountain, when a new granite and bronze bowl was installed and water reconnected.

HAMPSTEAD GENERAL HOSPITAL, NOW THE ROYAL FREE HOSPITAL

THE HAMPSTEAD GENERAL Hospital began as the Hampstead Home Hospital and Nursing Institute. Opened in May 1882 by Dr William Heath Strange, it was accommodated in a rented house – No. 4 Parliament Hill Road. The aim was to provide care for people who didn't want to go into a public hospital and could afford to pay towards their treatment. More houses were leased and, by 1894, it had twenty-nine beds and changed its name to the Hampstead Hospital.

But space was limited and in 1902 the foundation stone of the new Hampstead General Hospital was laid on the site of Bartrams Lodge, Haverstock Hill, once the home of Sir Rowland Hill, originator of the Penny Post. Hampstead General was designed by Keith Downes Young (who also worked on New End Hospital); the postcard shows the view from Hampstead Green. It opened in 1905 and when finances became stretched, extra funding was secured on condition that Hampstead merged with the North-West London Hospital in Camden Town, becoming the Hampstead General and North-West London Hospital. It was the first general hospital in London to own a motor ambulance, donated in 1913 by His Imperial Highness the Grand Duke Michael of Russia, who lived at Kenwood House.

In 1828, the Royal Free Hospital started as a free dispensary, opened by Dr William Marsden at No. 16 Greville Street, Hatton Garden. It moved to Grays Inn Road in 1842.

After the creation of the National Health Service in 1948, Hampstead General became part of the Royal Free Group. In 1957, the Ministry of Health announced that a new Royal Free Hospital and medical school should be built in Hampstead. Work finally got underway in 1968, and the first stage was completed six years later. Further work involved demolishing Hampstead General Hospital in 1975, its site being used for a car park and a garden dedicated to Dr Heath Strange. Queen Elizabeth II officially opened the hospital in 1978. Today, around 750,000 patients are seen every year at the hospital, with its huge range of general and specialist services. The modern photograph shows the main entrance on Pond Street. Based on a cruciform tower, its bulk is often criticised, in particular for spoiling the view from Hampstead Heath, although local objections secured a reduction in height.

LYNDHURST ROAD CONGREGATIONAL CHURCH AND AIR STUDIOS

THE CHURCH BEGAN in a temporary iron building in Willoughby Road in 1876. Robert Forman Horton, a charismatic young Oxford graduate, was invited to preach. The congregation numbered 220 by 1883 and sometimes there were as many as 600 people in a building designed to hold 440. Four wealthy members of the church bought a plot of land, selling on part of it to finance the building of the massive hexagonal church at the corner of Rosslyn Hill and Lyndhurst Road. Designed by Alfred Waterhouse, it cost around £20,000 and was opened in July 1884 with seating for 1,150 people. Pevsner calls it

'one of his most satisfactory works', where pulpit and organ faced the entrance, with deep galleries on three sides. Horton became the full-time minister, staying for nearly fifty years, until 1930. He was an influential writer and his Sunday night lectures attracted many working men. Horton's autobiography was commissioned on the spot by publisher Stanley Unwin, minutes after the latter had been married in the church.

The poet Stephen Spender recalled that as a child he was often dragged along to hear his father Harold lecture at the church. Harold suddenly stopped attending in 1918, after the Revd Horton (then in his 60s) married 26-year-old chorister Isobel Basden. According to family legend, she had rebounded into the minister's arms after nursing an unrequited affection for Harold. Horton died in 1934 at Christchurch Hill, Hampstead. In 1972 the church became United Reformed when the Presbyterian and Congregational churches merged. Its congregation moved to St Andrew's, Finchley Road, when the church closed in 1978 and became Lyndhurst Hall.

Today, the Associated Independent Recording (AIR) Studios are in the old church building. Sir George Martin, the Beatles' producer, set up the company in central London in 1969 and it took over Lyndhurst Hall in 1991. The interior was altered to provide a performance space and recording studios, opened in December 1992. Richard Boote bought AIR in February 2006, but it was up for sale again in 2012. Along with the music for many films, just a few of the famous artists who have recorded at Lyndhurst Road include Eric Clapton, Elton John, Madonna, Oasis, Paul McCartney and Robbie Williams.

BELSIZE HOUSE

BELSIZE HOUSE HAD a long history (*bel assis* means 'beautifully situated' in French); rebuilt several times with a succession of owners and occupiers, the illustration shows the house in the eighteenth century. It stood close to the present junction of Belsize Park Gardens, Belsize Avenue and Belsize Park, with distinctive hexagonal-shaped grounds. About 1704, Charles Povey rented the property from the 2nd Earl of Chesterfield, transforming Belsize House into a popular resort. Povey was an opportunistic businessman who established the Sun Insurance Company in 1708 and ran a private letter-carrying service before he was prosecuted by the Post Office. He opened the house and gardens to the public, offering a quick marriage in a private chapel for 5s, on condition that the wedding dinner was held in the gardens.

The increasing popularity of Belsize contributed to the decline of the first Hampstead Wells, after James Howell took over around 1720. Howell's advertising predicted that 'this undertaking will exceed all of the kind that has hitherto been known near London'. The Prince and Princess of Wales paid a visit in 1721 and on a single day in June 1722 it was claimed over 300 carriages travelled to Belsize, packed with pleasure seekers. Open from 6 a.m. to 8 p.m., there was music, dancing, gambling and deer and duck hunting, while secluded areas in the garden allowed visitors to indulge in illicit lovemaking. Horse

and foot races were regularly held, when footmen competed for a prize of six guineas.
Like Hampstead Wells before it, Belsize House increasingly attracted the wrong sort
of visitor and fell out of fashion. The resort was still open in the 1740s offering fewer
amusements, but after the house was rebuilt in 1745, it reverted to a private residence.
Spencer Perceval lived here for nine years. He called it 'a miserable hole' and embarked
on renovations and improvements. In 1812 he became the only prime minister to be
assassinated when he was shot by John Bellingham in the Houses of Parliament.

In 1807 the Chesterfield family sold their 234-acre Belsize estate, including Belsize
House and grounds. The modern photo looks down the present Belsize Avenue, the
original approach to Belsize House, which was demolished in 1853. The bricks were used
as foundations for the new roads, and the builder Daniel Tidey was responsible for many
of today's houses.

HAMPSTEAD TOWN HALL, HAVERSTOCK HILL

FOR MANY YEARS, the Hampstead Vestry, which later became the council, met at the workhouse in New End, until the decision was taken to erect the building shown here, which became Hampstead Town Hall. The site at the corner of Haverstock Hill and Belsize Avenue was acquired in March 1876 and the building was completed by William Shepherd, to the designs of H.E. Kendall and F. Mew. 'Erected AD 1877' appears on the exterior of the building, which opened in June 1878 at a cost of £18,500. This included £2,800 for the freehold of the site (the total is equivalent to about £1.5 million today). The design was praised at the time, but dismissed by Pevsner in his *Buildings of England* as 'crushingly mean'.

British Pathé has footage of Queen Victoria's Rifles (Territorials) in 1931, marching past the Mayor of Hampstead, on the steps of the Town Hall. Oswald Mosley's Fascists held a rally here in October 1936. John Parkhurst, journalist for the *Ham & High*, reported on the scene: 'A blackshirted figure stood in the centre of the platform flanked by a bodyguard.

William Joyce, Mosley's director of propaganda, was ranting at the Communists and the Jews. It was a sickening and alarming spectacle with young thugs pouncing on interrupters and bundling them down the staircase.' Fights broke out inside and outside the Town Hall and they were never allowed to hire the hall again.

In more recent times, annual arts festivals and exhibitions have been held at the hall as well as choral performances and tea dances. T.S. Eliot married Vivienne Haigh-Wood at the registry office here in June 1915, and comedian Dudley Moore and Suzy Kendall had a quiet marriage in June 1968. The Town Hall also featured in the 1994 film *Four Weddings and a Funeral*.

Plans for a new town hall at Swiss Cottage were abandoned when Hampstead became part of the larger Borough of Camden. Hampstead Town Hall was used by Camden until 1994, when it was declared 'surplus to requirements'. Local residents managed to get the building Grade II listed, and a bid to secure lottery funding to restore the Town Hall for community use was successful. Since the hall reopened in 2000, numerous concerts and other activities for the public have been held there. Interchange Studios, providing specialist facilities for young people and the disabled, and the University of the Third Age (Hampstead) offering many courses and talks, are both based here.

HAVERSTOCK HILL AND THE LOAD OF HAY PUBLIC HOUSE

THIS POSTCARD LOOKS north up Haverstock Hill, with a horse and cart waiting outside the Load of Hay pub. A stop for coaches on their way up and down the steep hill, the pub had a fashionable tea garden in the eighteenth century, the entrance guarded by two cut-out grenadiers, painted on flat boards. The most famous landlord was Joe Davis, 'the Host of Haverstock Hill'. A huge man who dressed eccentrically and was generally drunk, Davis was an attraction in his own right. One evening in March 1806 and the worse for drink, he threw himself on to the bar, as he often did. No one took any notice until closing time, when he was found to be dead.

In 1712, the writer Sir Richard Steele was living in a cottage opposite. The American author Washington Irving stayed at the cottage in 1824 and in *Tales of a Traveller*, he described the Irish

haymakers and drovers who regularly drank at the Load of Hay. In 1863, the 'picturesque wooden structure' was demolished and replaced by the current pub, one observer dismissing the new building as a 'suburban gin-palace'. Note the large lanterns outside, which were typical of the late Victorian era. Locally, Sir Richard Steele lent his name to another gin palace (the last building in the terrace on the left), Steele's Mews and Steele's Road.

In 1965, the Load of Hay was renamed the Noble Art due to the British Boxing Board of Control's new gymnasium behind the pub. Opened on 12 April by the Mayor of Camden, the premises were given rent-free by the brewers, for seven years. Henry Cooper trained there, as did Muhammad Ali for his fight against Brian London in August 1966. The gym also sparked a revival of Belsize Boxing Club, founded in 1880 at the Eyre Arms in St John's Wood.

The pub was reinstated as the Load of Hay in 1974 and Grade II listed. The name of the pub still appears at roof level with the date 1863, but today it's The Hill Bar and Brasserie, No. 94 Haverstock Hill, which opened in 2002. The upper floors have been converted to private housing, as has the remodelled gymnasium in the adjacent Hay Mews. And as the sign on a nearby lamppost proclaims, the area has been given the new identity of 'Steele's Village.'

ENGLAND'S LANE

THIS EARLY TWENTIETH-CENTURY view of England's Lane looks east from
the Washington pub at the corner of Belsize Park Gardens. Like the nearby Load of Hay,
it has impressive external lanterns. Originally a track leading to Upper Chalcots Farm,
the tenant in 1776 was James England, who lent his name to the lane. Building began
with two large houses, North Hall and Wychcombe, the latter on the southern corner
with Haverstock Hill. This became a boys' school, attended by writer Weedon Grossmith,
and described as 'a fine old house standing in its own grounds'. These two properties later
provided the site for Wychcombe Studios, home to many well-known artists.

In 1862, the eastern end of the lane ended in open fields, where Hampstead Cricket
Club played for many years. But development was just round the corner, in the hands
of Daniel Tidey. He built so many properties in and around England's Lane that the area

was nicknamed 'Tidey-Town'. The Washington pub dates from around 1865. Often said to be named after George Washington, for many years his portrait was on the pub sign. It was in fact Tidey's way of commemorating his birthplace, the Sussex village of Washington, and he was the first publican. He also built the shops in England's Lane, which developed into a busy commercial centre.

The attractive houses in Chalcot Gardens are set back from the south side of the lane behind a wall (and the trees on the postcard). The outstanding book illustrator Arthur Rackham lived at No. 16 (blue plaque) after his marriage to fellow artist Edyth Starkie in 1903, where they stayed until 1920. Both had previously occupied separate properties in Wychcombe Studios.

For a few years, No. 11 was the vicarage of St Mary's church on Primrose Hill Road. The vicar's son recalled the early twentieth century, when England's Lane had an 'excellent sweetshop' and the chemist (a branch of Stamp's in Hampstead High Street) sold leeches, storing them in glass jars.

The road remains a bustling retail centre, and coincidentally, the present landlord of the pub, Terry Tidey, is a relative of the nineteenth-century builder.

BELSIZE LIBRARY

BELSIZE BRANCH LIBRARY, on the corner of Antrim Road and Antrim Grove was the second public library to be opened by Hampstead Vestry. There were no architect's fees, as the building was designed by vestry surveyor Charles Lowe and chief librarian William Elliott Doubleday, to provide lending and reference sections, as well as a magazine room. At a well-attended ceremony, the foundation stone was laid on 10 August 1896, although the official opening in April 1897 was delayed by a strike.

Author Peter Vansittart (born 1920) was living nearby on Haverstock Hill when he made good use of the 'ill-lit' library as an 11-year-old schoolboy. 'It was my pidgin university. Each volume was bound in identical black. Thus I chose at random: Werfel, Buchan, Dumas, Merejowski, Cardus, Wodehouse. They made life dramatic in a new way.'

Unfortunately, any savings made by the vestry were wiped out when so many structural defects were found that the library had to close in 1936. A new building was commissioned from architects Hugh Andrew Gold and Rowland de Winton Aldridge and this time a reinforced concrete raft was laid. Compared with its predecessor, the present library looks very modern, 'progressively simple', and was described in the *Architects' Journal* as 'one of the best buildings of its kind in England'. Opened in March 1937, it was laid out as a single room to make for easy supervision by staff, with a tall, semi-circular window at one end. All furniture and fittings were made from English oak. A report in 1959 shows this was the busiest library in Hampstead, with 264,436 loans in the year.

By 1991, there were threats of closure and in 2012 Belsize Library did indeed shut, one of three libraries axed by Camden Council to save money. Following public pressure, it was reopened in June 2012 as Belsize Community Library, run by the Winchester Project.

BELSIZE CRESCENT

BELSIZE CRESCENT WAS known as Prince Consort Road until 1873. This view looks up the crescent from Belsize Lane with a horse and rider leisurely descending the hill. Much of the immediate area known as Belsize Village was developed by Daniel Tidey, a major operator capable of building fifty houses in a single year. His best were large and spacious; the typical white stucco Belsize Park property aimed at wealthy professional and middle-class tenants, looking for at least eight bedrooms. After going bankrupt, Tidey moved to Belsize Tavern, where his daughter was the licensee, in the 1870s and it remained his home until he died in 1885. Today, Belsize Tavern is a restaurant.

The building on the left was Burdett's office. William Burdett walked to London from Stamford to start a jobmasters, hiring carriages and horses, and then ran a carriage-making firm here. His son and grandson continued the business, which became a garage.

After the First World War, the large Belsize Park houses were subdivided, this process accelerating after the Second World War, when many were in very poor condition. In the 1950s, believing decline would continue, freeholders sold all their properties in Belsize Crescent. However, the 1960s and '70s saw the start of gentrification. Lesley Hornby, better known as the model and actress Twiggy, lived at No. 20. Other residents were guitarist Richard Thompson and Jeff Banks, the fashion designer. In the 1960s, The Witches' Cauldron at No. 50 Belsize Lane was a well-known coffee house and blues club. Belsize Lane became and still is a local shopping centre.

WINCHESTER ROAD

THE POSTCARD LOOKS south down Winchester Road, towards Adelaide Road. It was a street of comfortable villas, with the Winchester Hotel and public house, plus a short terrace of shops. Karl Blind, a German revolutionary and writer, lived at No. 3 from 1866 until his death in 1907. Around the time he moved here from St John's Wood, his stepson attempted to assassinate Bismarck and later committed suicide in custody. Blind's house became a meeting place for political refugees: 'If any interesting man came, especially from Germany, we were sure to meet him at one of those Sunday evenings in Winchester Road.' (Moncure D. Conway, *Autobiography*, 1904.) Although builders feared a church school would devalue property in the road, a site near the Hampstead Conservatoire was leased in 1873 to build St Paul's School. In 1881, South Hampstead High School (then St John's Wood High School) opened in a pair of semi-detached villas, Nos 13 and 15. The school left for Maresfield Gardens in 1882; St Paul's School moved to new premises by Primrose Hill in 1972, its site now occupied by sheltered housing.

In the late 1950s, Hampstead Council identified the area between Avenue Road and Winchester Road as the site for a new civic centre, including a library, swimming baths and town hall. Nos 22–32 north of Fellows Road, the pub and shops survived, but all the other buildings in Winchester Road were demolished.

The library and baths, designed by Sir Basil Spence, were opened by the Queen on 10 November 1964, and Hampstead Theatre opened in a temporary building. But further civic development was halted and some of the site sold off, when Hampstead became part of the Borough of Camden in 1965. Redevelopment of the east side of Winchester Road dates from around 1965, with plans for Taplow, a tower block at the corner of Adelaide Road, part of the regeneration of the surrounding area. Hampstead Theatre moved into its new state-of-the-art building on Eton Avenue in 2003. By 2007 all work was complete, including a makeover of the Grade II listed library, a new leisure centre by Sir Terry Farrell, affordable housing, community centre and The Visage, a block of private flats (on the right). The pub now houses 'The Winchester Project', working with young people. The tall building in the distance is the recently completed UCL Academy.

THE HAMPSTEAD CONSERVATOIRE AND CENTRAL SCHOOL, ETON AVENUE

GEORGE FRANCIS GEAUSSENT, a music professor, founded the Hampstead Conservatoire of Music in 1883. It began at No. 29 Belsize Crescent and moved to the building shown here, which opened in 1888. In 1893, Geaussent was accused of committing adultery at the Conservatoire with Annie Johnson, the mother of one of his pupils. Despite being represented by the charismatic barrister Marshall Hall, her husband's case was dismissed. Geaussent retired in 1896 to run his Belfast Conservatoire. The musical heyday of the

Conservatoire was from 1896 to 1905, under the guidance of Cecil Sharp, the next principal.

The Conservatoire's hall was hired for bazaars, political meetings, lectures and classes. Beatrice Curtis Brown had dancing lessons there when she was a child. She recalled: 'Little girls trooped up the steps from the street decorously. When we had changed our shoes we gathered in a high, chilly hall, our mothers and nurses ranked themselves on the platform behind the pianist. We were drilled by a fine grey-haired old lady in black silk who had the stature and poise of a duchess. We did exercises, pointing toes, taking up the "positions", all to sprightly little tunes.' In 1918, Sir Ernest Shackleton was booked, to 'tell the thrilling story of the Antarctic Expedition', illustrated by 'magnificent lantern slides'.

The Conservatoire was put up for sale in 1927 and described as 'suitable for conversion into a cinema or theatre'. The Embassy Theatre soon opened here, in September 1928. In 1954, the owner went bankrupt and the theatre was bought by the Central School of Speech and Drama in 1956. Central School, formed in 1906, had moved from the Albert Hall. Famous pupils have included Laurence Olivier, Vanessa Redgrave, Judi Dench, Harold Pinter, Dawn French and Jennifer Saunders. Today's building has modern extensions to left and right. In 2012, the Queen approved the title 'Royal Central School of Speech and Drama' in recognition of its world-class reputation.

THE SWISS COTTAGE TAVERN

IN 1826, AN Act of Parliament sanctioned the building of
Avenue Road and Finchley (New) Road, which was open by the early
1830s. This postcard looks north across Finchley Road to the Swiss
Cottage Tavern (behind the wall), and beyond it to the Swiss Cottage
Dairy. Avenue Road ran behind these premises. By 1856 this was a
busy bus terminus and the Underground station opened in 1868.

The Swiss Cottage Tavern was built in the late 1830s in the popular
'Swiss chalet' style. Unfortunately, an early news report of the pub in
June 1839 concerned William Mack, a 20-year-old haymaker, who was
found dead in a barn on Haverstock Hill, having drunk a pint and a half
of raw spirit at the tavern. An ex-pugilist, Frank Redmond, was the first
landlord and the pub became a popular meeting place for runners and
competitive walkers, who used the Finchley Road for their races. In 1842,
an estimated 4,000 people watched a race over a quarter of a mile,
the winner covering the distance in fifty-six seconds.

In 1845, the whole of London was talking about the murder of 29-year-old James Delarue, found dead in a field near Belsize House. His friend Thomas Hocker claimed he was drinking in the Swiss Cottage Tavern at the time, and he concocted an elaborate story to explain Delarue's death. But the Old Bailey jury found Hocker guilty of murder and he was hanged on 28 April 1845.

The tavern gave its name to the surrounding area and has been rebuilt several times. It became simply The Swiss Cottage and was renamed Ye Olde Swiss Cottage in the late 1920s. The pub was sold in 1948 for £176,000 and rebuilt in 1966, the same year the decision was taken to make Finchley Road into a six-lane highway.

The Swiss Cottage Dairy (established 1849) was built north of the tavern, with a 'long, thatched roof and quaint little windows, in one of which was always a basket of eggs'. The dairy and tavern, with 'large pleasure grounds and extensive stabling' were for sale in 1881, the latter occupied for many years by William Burdett, the jobmaster from Belsize Crescent. The dairy closed in 1927.

The Odeon Cinema was opened on 4 September 1937 by the Mayor of Hampstead, with guests including the director Alexander Korda and film star Merle Oberon.

The modern building in today's photograph, beyond the traffic lights, is part of the Royal Central School of Speech and Drama on the corner with Eton Avenue.
No. 100 Avenue Road, a mix of offices and restaurants, rises behind the pub.

JOHN BARNES
DEPARTMENT STORE,
FINCHLEY ROAD

THE TRADERS IN Hampstead High Street would not have enjoyed reading the
newspaper reports announcing that London's latest emporium, 'John Barnes & Co.'
had opened in Finchley Road on 29 March 1900. The company was set up by a
syndicate, but chairman John Barnes died in the sinking of the *Stella* off Guernsey
in 1899 with considerable loss of life. The postcard shows the store filling an island
site south of Finchley Road station. The aim was to attract middle-class residents by
providing a lavishly equipped shop with thirty-seven departments and a staff of almost
400. 'The establishment has been fitted up with an especial view to the comfort and
convenience of customers, selling the best merchandise the world can produce at its

lowest cost.' Local traders were right to be worried; in the words of a customer, 'John Barnes had virtually everything'.

When Selfridges took over John Barnes in 1926, annual sales were well over £250,000. They rebuilt, commissioning architect T.P. Bennett to design the building pictured today, adding five storeys of residential flats above three floors of retail space. Demolition began in 1932, with the new shop completed in two phases, in 1936 and 1938. The Mayor of Hampstead believed rebuilding John Barnes would make Finchley Road 'the Regent Street of north London'.

In 1938, author John Trewin moved to Fitzjohn's Avenue and opened an account at John Barnes. His wife Wendy was surprised by the goods on offer: 'There were fruit and vegetables I had never seen before; there was a Kosher display, and the grocery shelves held tins of lichees and passion-fruit among the familiar peaches and pineapple chunks. The delicatessen department had an infinitely larger repertoire than the cooked-meat shops I had known ... The customers spoke a variety of languages chiefly middle European, a flood of foreign tongues came towards you from the restaurant, and on the pavement outside women who had recently fled from Nazism and settled in Swiss Cottage or West Hampstead talked to compatriots.'

The company was acquired by the John Lewis Partnership in 1940, who tried unsuccessfully to sell the Finchley Road store in the 1960s. The opening of Brent Cross Shopping Centre in the 1970s led to a further reduction in trade. Despite local protests, John Barnes closed in 1981. Today, the ground floor is occupied by a Waitrose supermarket.

THE O2 CENTRE, FINCHLEY ROAD

THIS 1939 PHOTO shows Finchley Road, from the Underground station (extreme left) as far as No. 261. An early trader was Thomas Fall, an important photographer who specialised in portraits of dogs and worked extensively for Crufts. From left to right, beyond the white awning, the shops are the Gas Light & Coke Company (opened in 1927), Randall butchers, Green & Edwards (a drapers and house furnishers that occupied Nos 241–253), grocers Teetgen & Co, Glasscraft, Randall bootmakers and Ganter jewellers.

The parade eventually became run down. Writer Patrice Chaplin lived in a flat off the main road and described Finchley Road between John Barnes and Arkwright Road (which included this parade) as, 'shifty, shiftless, squalid, dirty, uncertain. Shops are there one day, gone the next.'

In October 1993, over a period of eight days, the IRA left a series of Semtex bombs in various London locations, three of which exploded in the Finchley Road. Luckily nobody was killed, but six people were injured by flying glass. Derek Doherty, aged 23, and Gerard Mackin, 33, were found guilty of planting the bombs and jailed for twenty-five years each.

All the premises north of No. 239 now lie under the O2 Centre, which opened in 1998. Behind the Finchley Road frontage, the site stretches back almost as far as West End Lane. This land comprised derelict railway sidings and there had been several proposals how best to redevelop it. Buildings on Finchley Road were demolished in the early 1990s in preparation for the centre, but problems with planning permission and concern over traffic led to construction being delayed. In 1995, the Burford Group delivered brochures to 15,000 households and 400 businesses, inviting people to choose between three suggestions for the site and also to name the development. But there was no clear majority for any of the plans, while comments were evenly split between those wanting a modern approach and those wishing the scheme to be more traditional. So a fourth design was submitted to Camden Council, which addressed such aspects as height differences between existing properties and the new centre, with greater use of brick and reconstituted stone, to better blend with the streetscape. The original £15m budget was exceeded by early 1997, causing a temporary delay until additional capital investors could be found. Currently, parts of the centre are being remodelled.

SOUTH HAMPSTEAD HIGH SCHOOL, MARESFIELD GARDENS

SOUTH HAMPSTEAD HIGH School for Girls (SHHS) began in Winchester Road,
the ninth school run by the Girls' Public Day School Company (later Trust). The 'able
government' of headmistress Rebecca Allen Olney ensured it was soon over subscribed.
Needing more space, the 'comely' building at No. 3 Maresfield Gardens was designed by
E.C. Robins, to accommodate 300 pupils. Shown on the postcard, the school was opened
on 13 May 1882 by Princess Louise, President of the National Union for Improving the
Education of Women. The 1904 prospectus advertised morning and optional afternoon

© Hopkins Architects

sessions. Fees ranged from £3 10s to £5 10s per term, depending on age.
In 1910, the girls raised £3 3s for a sled dog to accompany Captain Scott on
his expedition to the South Pole. The 1948 film *Scott of the Antarctic* includes
a scene where a pupil hands over the money. Muriel Grainger joined SHHS as
a pupil in 1918 and coming from a smaller school, described 'so much more
of everything, more girls, more classrooms, more noise'. She was taught for
a term by author Dorothy L. Sayers, standing-in for a sick English teacher.
There was a wartime paper shortage and when slates were introduced, they
were so cold that the girls got chilblains down the sides of their hands.

After the death of artist Sir Ernest Waterlow in 1919, the school took
over and later demolished his house, No. 1 Maresfield Gardens, building
Waterlow Hall in its place. During the Second World War, the girls were
evacuated and the school was used as a fire station. The poet Stephen
Spender joined the auxiliary fire service and lived in a flat next door.
In 1944, sheltering in the basement, he recalled a 'rushing noise like
a train coming down a vertical tunnel through the sky ... a great thud,
our room rocked, followed by the sound of things collapsing'. A bomb
had fallen about 100 yards away, bringing down the ceiling. In 2010,
the architects behind the London Olympic Velodrome published plans for
a radical redevelopment of the entire site (pictured here). Involving the
construction of new buildings, selected renovation, and the excavation of
an underground sports hall, the new school is due to open in 2014. Among
the many distinguished old girls are Rabbi Julia Neuberger, author Fay
Weldon and actresses Helena Bonham Carter and Dame Angela Lansbury.

SHEPHERD'S WELL

SHEPHERD'S WELL OR The Conduit was the source of a branch of the Tyburn River.
For many years it was also the main provider of drinking water for Hampstead, because
it tasted pleasant. Before piped water, residents got water from ponds, wells or springs.
But much of Hampstead's water was impregnated with iron and tasted nasty, hence the
popularity of this well, in the fields between Swiss Cottage and Hampstead. If you could
afford to pay, the water was brought to your door. A report from the 1840s commented
on this industry. 'At this place men may be seen occupied at all hours of the day filling
their pails with water, which they sell to the inhabitants.' The picture of 1827 shows
the site to be very exposed, lending weight to a complaint that the well mouth collected

rubbish and should be protected. In 1833, the average yield was
estimated at 10 tons per hour, but in summer the well could almost
run dry. Carriers, therefore, worked through the night: 'At times,
in the hot weather, this spring becomes so nearly exhausted that the
carriers are obliged to wait for the water rising, and fill their pails
by means of common earthenware basins, which the carriers call
dippers.' The water carriers had a yoke and two buckets. The cost
of a pail depended on distance from the well: 2d in the town and
up to 3d beyond. One water carrier known as Jack Rough 'worked
from morning to night, carrying his full buckets to his various
customers in the town; crooning some popular ditty to himself as he
went along, swinging his pendant buckets in time with the tune he
was humming'.

In 1856, the New River Company built their reservoir in
Hampstead Grove. Piped water was laid on to many households and
Shepherd's Well became increasingly neglected: 'the whole spot is
filthy and disreputable' (1869). In the mid-1870s, Fitzjohn's Avenue
was laid across the fields to Hampstead and, in 1878, Shepherd's Well
disappeared. As the modern photograph shows, a drinking fountain
was installed on the wall of No. 68 Fitzjohn's Avenue, close to the
site of the old well at the junction of Akenside and Lyndhurst Road.
It was removed in 1988 after being repeatedly vandalised.

WELLS BUILDINGS, ORIEL PLACE

THIS POSTCARD SHOWS the patriotic decorations displayed by tenants of Wells Buildings, Oriel Place to celebrate George V's coronation in 1911. The block was built on the site of Crockett's Court, a slum cul-de-sac off Hampstead High Street. In about 1875, Hampstead Wells Trust bought the property to redevelop as working-class housing. It was home to ninety-five people, fifty-four of them children; few, if any, were rehoused in the new Wells Buildings. Designed by Henry Simpson Legg and completed in 1876, the first tenants moved in on 19 March 1877. Charles Booth in his *Survey of London* considered the buildings 'tall and gloomy', but they were a healthy place to live and well ventilated with open staircases. The weekly rent for a tenement of one, two or three rooms was 3s 6d, 5s 6d and 7s respectively. There was a club room on the ground floor, a laundry on the top floor and drying space on the roof. The trustees also created a garden opposite the block. In 1894, Frederick Windsor, aged 10, was charged with stealing 2s 6d from his parents who lived in the Buildings. Previously convicted for stealing £2 from them, he was sent to an industrial school until he was 16 years old.

The club room was rented to various organisations, including a Penny (Savings) Bank, started by a couple of local residents in 1879, and held every Saturday evening for forty-five years. In 1901, metered gas was laid on to the Buildings, but none of the occupants wanted electricity (which was finally installed in 1933). By the 1950s, it was obvious that the flats needed updating, to include a proper kitchen, bath, sink and toilet, but the Trust lacked the funds to carry out the work. In 1963, the flats failed Hampstead Council's standards for buildings in multiple occupation and three years later Camden Council agreed to take them over, paying the Trust £6,000. Renamed Wells Court, the 'healthy' open staircases were enclosed and the flats modernised. Today they provide sheltered housing. (The estate agent sign in the old postcard displays the name Goldschmidt and Howland, which opened in 1888 and is still trading.)

CHURCH ROW

PEVSNER IN HIS *Buildings of England* calls Church Row
'the best street in Hampstead'. Building here was
stimulated by the success of Hampstead Wells; most
houses date from the eighteenth century and retain
a wealth of Georgian detail. The road leads to the
parish church of St John, rebuilt in 1747. This picture
shows a promenade in Church Row, which became a
fashionable place to visit. The church was enlarged
and reoriented in 1878, with the altar at the west end.
The churchyard (original ground and the extension) is
divided by Church Row. Artist John Constable (*d.* 1837)
is probably the most famous person buried here.
Several of the Hampstead residents mentioned in this
book are also here: the Revd Allatson Burgh (of Burgh
House); Philip Fenton (of Fenton House); Edward
Stamp (chemist, No. 29 High Street), and Daniel Tidey
(builder and publican), as well as a plot set aside for
the Royal Soldiers' Daughters' Home. In 1845, several
hundred onlookers watched the funeral of murder
victim James Delarue.

Church Row has been home to many famous people. The singer Dame Gracie Fields was a tenant in the 1930s, and authors Ernest and Diana Raymond rented a top-floor flat in August 1940. Poet and editor John James Park was at No. 18; his son Thomas was just 19 years old when he wrote the first history of Hampstead in 1814. Writer and cartoonist George du Maurier occupied No. 27 from 1870 to 1874, where his son Sir Gerald, the actor-manager, was born. They too are buried in the churchyard. Lord Alfred Douglas, Oscar Wilde's 'Bosie', was living with his wife at No. 26 in 1907. In 1909, No. 17 was the home of H.G. Wells, or rather his family, as Wells was living with his mistress Amber Reeves. In 1965, the house was bought for £24,000 by comedian Peter Cook. He and Dudley Moore worked on the top floor. Peter and his wife Wendy held numerous dinner parties in the basement kitchen with guests such as Peter Ustinov, John Lennon and Paul McCartney. Peter Cook sold the house for £45,000 in 1971, but he liked Hampstead and two years later he moved to Perrin's Court with his second wife Judy Huxtable.

CHURCH ROW TOLL GATE

THIS PHOTOGRAPH, TAKEN about 1900, looks west along Church Row, with the churchyard railings (left) and the corner of Frognal Gardens (right). Mrs Christiana Bullock, wife of gardener Henry Bullock, is standing outside their cottage. This was built on the Old Mansion estate, which extended from Frognal across to Holly Hill and Church Row. The Old Mansion (now No. 94 Frognal) owned the rights to the toll gate across Church Row and it was legal to charge a fee to pass through the gate; the Bullocks' cottage doubled as the gardener's home and tollbooth.

Cornelius Patrick Sulivan moved into the Old Mansion in the 1820s. His daughter Mary died there in 1887 when the estate was bought by civil engineer Alexander Gray, who laid out Frognal Gardens from 1890, across part of the grounds. Mary Sulivan had steadfastly refused to relinquish ownership of the toll gate: 'It was her right, and she resolved not to abate an iota of her power; so the struggle became continuous.' (Caroline White, *Sweet Hampstead*, 1900.) The gate was closed on every Ascension Day and no one allowed through, in an effort to prove the private ownership of this part of Church Row.

In 1900, it still cost 1*d* to pass through the gate and many avoided it; tradesmen were charged 6*d* a week for unlimited passage. In August 1903, the local paper reported that the toll gate had been removed and the cottage demolished. Its site lies partly under today's wide pavement at the entrance to Frognal Gardens. Later that year, Hampstead residents sent a petition to the council, 'calling attention to the largely increased traffic through Church Row since the removal of the toll gate' and asking for the road to be widened at that point. No. 1 Frognal Gardens (on the right), which now forms the corner property with Church Row, has been described as a 'flamboyant Gothic style house' designed by Thomas Worthington of Manchester for Henry John Robberds Herford. Herford was a civil servant and a talented woodcarver, decorating the large seventeen-room house with his own work. The Revd Brooke Herford, appointed minister at nearby Rossyln Chapel in 1892, was Henry's uncle. Henry carved a chimney piece for a schoolroom at the chapel, bearing the words 'Serve God and be Merry'. He lived at Frognal Gardens until his death in 1946.

HEATH STREET

THE IMAGE BELOW looks up Heath Street, across the junction with Holly Hill (left) and
Hampstead High Street (right). The purpose-built Hampstead fire station proudly flies
the Union Jack from its tower. Designed by George Vulliamy, it opened in 1873 on the
site of the former police station and used horse-drawn engines. Staff lived on the upper
floors: the 1901 census shows seven firemen, two coachmen and their families; a total of
thirty-eight people. The stables featured mechanical devices that lowered saddles on to the
horses' backs. Thomas Tilling's, a major omnibus company, provided the Metropolitan Fire
Brigade with specially selected horses that were strong enough to gallop while pulling an
engine and accustomed to street traffic.

David Lloyd George opened the Hampstead Underground station on 22 June 1907, from
Charing Cross via Camden Town to Golders Green or Highgate (today's Archway). As many
as 150,000 passengers travelled free that day. A spokesman declared the line 'opened up

Hampstead and Highgate, to which access had hitherto been somewhat inconvenient, and thus provided the people of London with new possibilities of living in the country'. Hampstead is the deepest station in London, some 192ft below street level. Leslie Green designed the stations to a standard format, with distinctive dark red-tiled exteriors. The vertical 'Underground' sign over the entrance was adopted in 1908.

The fire station tower was used as an observation post in the First World War, when a warning rocket fired from here unfortunately damaged the nearby Hampstead Parochial School. The station closed in 1923 and was bought by estate agents Hampton & Sons to use as their local office. Around 1928 the tower was reduced in height and the clock, bought by public subscription, still keeps good time today.

Hampstead's platforms display the original name proposed for the station, 'Heath Street'. During the Second World War, this deep station was in great demand as a shelter. An elderly widow from Malden Road was a regular; her husband had died from injuries after a bombing raid and she worried about spending Christmas away, in case she lost her place at the shelter. In September 1940, when novelist Ernest Raymond returned during a raid, he had to climb the 320-plus stairs to the booking hall. 'The walls turned slowly round, having no end. The bleak stone stairs grew, one from the other, leading only to more stairs.' Today, a secret garden behind the station, planted and tended by staff, is occasionally open to the public.

JACK STRAW'S CASTLE

THIS PHOTOGRAPH SHOWS Jack Straw's Castle in the 1920s, with the recently erected Hampstead Borough War Memorial in the foreground. No one knows how this well-known pub at the top of Hampstead got its name, which is first mentioned in 1713. Jack Straw was one of the leaders of the Peasant's Revolt, although it's almost certain he didn't come to Hampstead and there was never a castle nearby. But in the words of Thomas Barratt, the Hampstead historian, 'as to that we need not worry now, sufficient that it has been a house of call, festive gathering, tea-drinking, and holiday resort from early Georgian, perhaps Stuart days'. The pub was a favourite with Charles Dickens, who invited his biographer John Forster to dine there: 'You don't feel disposed, do you, to muffle yourself up and start off with me for a brisk walk over Hampstead Heath? I knows a good 'ouse where we can have a red-hot chop for dinner, with a glass of good wine.' Wilkie Collins, Karl Marx and Friedrich Engels were also regulars at the pub.

On 17 February 1856, the body of John Sadleir was found near Jack Straw's. He was an MP from Ireland who, after getting into financial difficulty, sold forged deeds and cheques. He committed suicide by swallowing a bottle of prussic acid.

Jack Straw's Castle was a popular venue for trippers visiting Hampstead, and 1930s plans to replace adjacent houses with blocks of flats never materialised. The pub was badly damaged by a landmine in 1941, which destroyed neighbouring properties. Their sites were added to the Heath and used for the car park behind the pub. Land was donated by a member of the Guinness family, who owned Heath House, and the Borough War Memorial was moved to its present site in front of the property in 1953, when it was also made commemorative of the Second World War. It has recently been restored.

The present Jack Straw's building by Raymond Erith was approved by the LCC in 1962, after many protests. Hampstead's Planning Committee particularly criticised the 'pseudo-historic' elevation and the wooden battlements. 'The Council would like to see a building as plain and simple as its predecessor, of modern design but without false trimmings.' After another planning battle, work got underway in 2003 to convert the Grade II-listed pub into residential accommodation, with commercial premises on the ground floor.

WHITESTONE POND

THIS POSTCARD LOOKS across Whitestone Pond to East Heath Road and Bell-Moor, the home of Thomas Barratt (1841–1914), soap millionaire and historian. Whitestone Pond is named after an old milestone at the end of Hampstead Grove. The original dew pond was enlarged and lined by the Hampstead Vestry in 1875 and artificially supplied with water in 1890. Ramps allowed carters to drive horse-drawn vehicles through the pond, refreshing their horses after the long climb up the hill.

This is the highest point in North London, 440ft above sea level and the site of a 1588 Armada beacon, intended to warn of Spanish invasion. In 1912, Barratt wrote: 'Ten counties are said to be visible on a clear day,' when visitors could pick out Windsor Castle, the grandstand at Epsom and Epping Forest. Whitestone Pond became the focus for day-trippers who came to drink at nearby Jack Straw's Castle, have a donkey ride,

sail toy boats on the pond or skate in winter. There were so many donkeys that George du Maurier nicknamed the Hampstead ponds, 'Ponds Asinorum'. The Salvation Army held regular concerts here. Meetings campaigning for women's votes attracted huge and often disruptive crowds who regularly threatened to throw the speakers into the pond.

Thomas Barratt was the son of a piano maker. In 1864 he joined the soap-making firm A&F Pears, marrying the boss's daughter the following year. Barratt recognised the power of advertising to sell product, most famously by adding a bar of Pears' soap to a Millais painting of a young boy blowing bubbles. Barratt bought four properties opposite Whitestone Pond (including Albion Cottage, Constable's first Hampstead home), and created the palatial Bell-Moor, where he lived from 1877 to 1914. Barratt completed his three-volume Hampstead history in 1912 and donated his archive to the council. His son sold Bell-Moor in 1928 and by October 1929, the site had been cleared. Original plans for a nine-storey building were reduced by the LCC to five. In 1931, rents started at £750 when eighteen 'super-flats' were marketed, each having '10 magnificent rooms with 3 bath rooms in addition'. Today the building is screened by trees.

The pond and its immediate environs were refurbished in 2010, with water planting, improved landscaping around the old milestone and a new seating area at the end of Hampstead Grove.

THE VALE OF
HEALTH HOTEL

THERE WAS ONLY a small cluster of properties in
the Vale of Health when poet Leigh Hunt rented
a cottage in 1815. John Keats was a frequent
visitor, as was Shelley: 'Here also he swam his
paper boats on the ponds, and delighted to play
with my children.' The Vale of Health Hotel
(pictured right) was promoted by Donald Nicoll
and opened in 1863, with the specific intention
of providing refreshment and entertainment to
trippers on a large scale, the number of visitors
having increased with the opening of Hampstead
Heath station. Visitors could sit on the veranda to
watch friends rowing on the pond or fishing. Built
as a reservoir, the pond and its muddy bottom
proved fatal to a number of swimmers and skaters.
In 1864, Nicoll rescued a boy who fell through the
ice but was unable to save his friend. The hotel was
rebuilt in 1904–05 and the upper floors converted
into studios. Artist Henry Lamb rented one
between 1912 and 1924, and was succeeded by

Stanley Spencer between 1924 and 1927. Spencer was mainly working on his 'Cookham Resurrection', which was so large that the studio windows had to be removed to get it out.

Stanley Spencer married Hilda Carline and their daughter, Shirin, was born in 1925. According to Kenneth Pople's biography of Spencer (1991), visitors to the studio would sometimes find Stanley washing nappies or holding the sleeping baby while continuing to paint the picture. His landlord Fred Gray also ran the Vale of Health fair, and caused a stir in 1926 by claiming a seal had been caught in the pond. He told a reporter, 'There is no doubt that there are other big creatures. On a fine day, from the veranda, we can see them.' Christened "Appy of 'Ampstead', a relative later admitted the seal left Hampstead the way it arrived; on the back of lorry. Camden Council eventually closed the hotel in 1960. Demolished in 1964, it was replaced by Spencer House, a block of flats. Residents remember fairs during weekends and summer on currently derelict land by the flats and where caravans are parked today, but they haven't been held for many years. Planning permission for both sites has been refused.

THE VIADUCT,
HAMPSTEAD HEATH

THE POSTCARD SHOWS the Viaduct on Hampstead Heath, with sheep grazing in the distance. Since 1829, Sir Thomas Maryon Wilson, Lord of the Manor of Hampstead, had been trying to get permission to build on Hampstead Heath. In 1844 he published a plan for twenty-eight villas on the East Park estate, fronting a road he built from the Vale of Health to Downshire Hill. It was carried across a valley by the Viaduct, where on 2 September 1845, a band entertained a large crowd as Sir Thomas and his sister arrived to lay the first block. The Viaduct was nicknamed 'Wilson's folly', because it took three years to complete due to the swampy ground. Sir Thomas never got his building permission. Instead, he exploited and damaged the Heath by digging out large amounts of sand and gravel on either side of Spaniards Road, supplying the Midland Railway for their

line to St Pancras. In about 1865 he granted a twenty-one-year lease to make bricks along the East Park estate road. The postcard shows the remains of the brick earth excavations to the right of the Viaduct. In 1871, there were ten makeshift cottages in the brickfields, housing sixty people.

The Viaduct and the road are still there, but as shown in today's photo, trees have grown and multiplied and now block the view. Sadly, the pond often featured in nineteenth-century reports of suicides. In 1896, 9-year-old Harry Orders fell into the water and was rescued by 12-year-old Egbert Perry, one of the youngest people to receive an award from the Royal Humane Society.

The sheep remained until around 1955. Both men and women looked after the livestock; the last shepherdess was a Mrs Mortimer. In the 1920s, George Donald lived in a hut near the Vale of Health for ten months each year looking after 200–1,000 sheep with the help of his Alsatian dog, Birk. The sheep were described as 'nervous', probably because they were so often chased by dogs and children. In 1880 a naturalist reported a kingfisher nesting by the pond and recently an artificial bank has been created upstream from the Viaduct in the hope that kingfishers will return.

KENWOOD HOUSE, HAMPSTEAD HEATH

IN 1754, THE 1st Earl of Mansfield bought Kenwood House as a country retreat.
He engaged James and Robert Adams, who built the entry porch on the north side,
remodelled the south front and added a magnificent library to balance the existing orangery.
The picture of 1785 shows the wall that originally separated the mansion from Hampstead
Lane. Kenwood House became Mansfield's home after his Bloomsbury mansion was
destroyed in 1780, during the Gordon Riots. The 2nd Earl was only here between 1793 and
1796, but turned Kenwood into a first-rate house. Architect George Saunders added the
music and dining room wings to the north front. He also added the service wing, stables,
dairy and rebuilt the farm. Humphry Repton was consulted on landscaping. Hampstead
Lane was rerouted to run on the other side of Prospect Hill in front of the house, allowing
removal of the wall and creation of a new driveway. From 1910–1917, Kenwood was let

by the 6th Earl to Grand Duke Michael, grandson of Tsar Nicholas of Russia, at an annual rent of £2,200. He enjoyed a lavish lifestyle, 'with big dogs and even bigger Circassian guards in glamorous uniforms patrolling the grounds'. Two dogs are buried, with gravestones, in North Wood. A keen sportsman, the Grand Duke opened the high-diving board at Highgate Ponds; British Pathé has clips of divers training there. He also allowed an anti-aircraft mobile battery to be based at Kenwood during the First World War.

The property acquired by the Earls of Mansfield forms a large part of what we today call Hampstead Heath. The first public acquisition was the Elms estate and Parliament Hill Fields adjoining the Maryon Wilson East Park estate, which the 4th Earl agreed to sell in 1889. But the 6th Earl hardly ever visited Kenwood House and in 1914 decided to dispose of the remaining 200 acres; 132 acres were secured for public use but Kenwood House and grounds remained at risk. In 1922, the mansion was emptied and a plan issued the following year, showing the property divided into thirty-three plots for villas. In 1925, Lord Iveagh (Edward Cecil Guinness) bought the entire estate for £107,900, worth over £5 million today. He died in 1927, having bequeathed the house and land to the public, along with his valuable collection of pictures.

In 1971, two Guardi paintings were stolen from Kenwood House and were later recovered in Belgium. A Vermeer was taken in February 1974. Following a tip-off, it was found a few weeks later in an east London graveyard. Kenwood House has recently undergone restoration by English Heritage.

If you enjoyed this book, you may also be interested in …

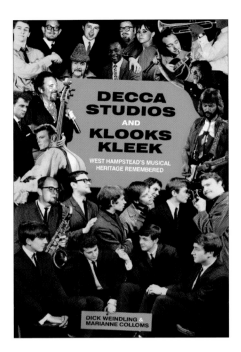

Decca Studios and Klooks Kleek
DICK WEINDLING & MARIANNE COLLOMS

The book explores the history of Decca Studios, where thousands of records were made between 1937 and 1980. Klooks Kleek was run next door from 1961 to 1970 in the Railway Hotel by Dick Jordan and Geoff Williams, who share their memories here. With artists including David Bowie, The Rolling Stones, Tom Jones and The Moody Blues at Decca, and Ronnie Scott, Cream, Fleetwood Mac, Led Zeppelin, Jimi Hendrix, Eric Clapton, Elton John, Rod Stewart and Stevie Wonder at Klooks, this book records a unique musical heritage. Containing more than fifty photographs, many of which have never before appeared in print, it will delight music lovers everywhere.

978 0 7509 5287 3

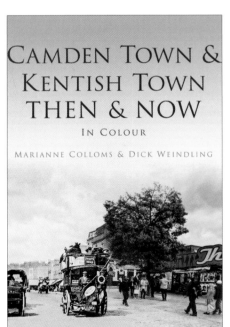

Camden Town & Kentish Town Then & Now
MARIANNE COLLOMS & DICK WEINDLING

Contrasting forty-five archive images alongside modern full-colour photographs, this book charts the evolution of Camden Town and Kentish Town over the centuries. Railways and piano making provided much employment, while residents' spiritual needs were well served by the many churches and chapels. Theatres and cinemas provided entertainment and almost anything could be purchased in the many shops in the area. Today, the area around Camden Lock has become one of London's leading tourist attractions, famous for its vibrant atmosphere. While much has changed, there is much of the old Camden Town and Kentish Town remaining, as can be seen here.

978 0 7524 7467 0

Visit our website and discover thousands of other History Press books.

www.thehistorypress.co.uk